THE SNOW GOOSE

BY
MARK E. AHLSTROM

*For Stoops, Lloyd, and Keith —
three special friends from
Nokomis, Saskatchewan*

EDITED BY
DR. HOWARD SCHROEDER
**Professor in Reading and Language Arts
Dept. of Elementary Education
Mankato State University**

PRODUCED AND DESIGNED BY
BAKER STREET PRODUCTIONS
Mankato, MN

CRESTWOOD HOUSE
Mankato, Minnesota

LIBRARY OF CONGRESS CATALOGING IN PUBLICATION DATA

Ahlstrom, Mark E.
  The snow goose.

  (Wildlife, habits & habitats)
  SUMMARY: Discusses the habits and behavior of North America's snow goose, a survivor of the Ice Age.
  1. Snow goose--Juvenile literature. (1. Snow goose. 2. Geese) I. Schroeder, Howard. II. Title. III. Series.
  QL696.A52A373   1985   598.4'1   85-29933
  ISBN 0-89686-293-3 (lib. bdg.)

International Standard
Book Number:
Library Binding 0-89686-293-3

Library of Congress
Catalog Card Number:
85-29933

ILLUSTRATION CREDITS:

John Gerlach/Tom Stack & Assoc.: Cover, 6
Gary R. Zahm/DRK Photo: 4-5, 18
Mark E. Ahlstrom: 9, 10, 22, 35, 36
Lynn Rogers: 14, 31
James Brandenburg: 17
Lynn M. Stone: 21, 27, 32, 39, 40, 43, 44
G.C. Kelley/Tom Stack & Assoc.: 24-25
Leonard Lee Rue III/Tom Stack & Assoc.: 28

Copyright© 1986 by Crestwood House, Inc. All rights reserved. No part of this book may be reproduced in any form without written permission from the publisher, except for brief passages included in a review. Printed in the United States of America.

Hwy. 66 South, Box 3427
Mankato, MN 56002-3427

TABLE OF CONTENTS

Introduction: 4
Chapter I: A general look at the snow goose 6
  A big family
  Geese have old ancestors
  Geese greet the first humans
  Finding names wasn't easy
  Ross' goose—a close relative
  The two types of snow geese
  White phase and blue phase
  Moves with the seasons
  Migration routes are changing
  Why snow geese migrate
  How do they get where they're going?
  Great navigators
  Breeding grounds of the lesser snow goose
  Breeding grounds of the greater snow goose
  Winter areas of the snow goose
Chapter II: A closer look at the snow goose 30
  Sharp senses
  Food and feeding habits
  Feeding habits change
  Migration habits change, too
  High flyers
  Spring is the time for mating
  Eggs are laid in June
  New feathers
  Enemies of the snow goose
  The outlook is good
Map 45
Index/Glossary ....46 - 47

INTRODUCTION:

I'm sure many people have seen flocks of snow geese fly overhead. The flocks are usually so high that they don't make much of an impression. I, for one, never thought much about the snow goose.

That all changed a couple of years ago when I found myself on the prairies of Saskatchewan. Some friends and I were there to do some duck and goose hunting in the fall. One morning we were waiting in a field to the west of Boulder Lake. We were in the field because we had seen some Canada geese feeding in the field the evening before. We hoped the geese might return to feed in the morning.

Thousands of snow geese lift off a lake.

We never did get a chance to shoot a goose, but we got a show that we will never forget.

The show began with a loud roar just at sunrise. At the time we didn't know what it was. Later, we figured it out. It was the roar of thousands of snow geese flying off the water of Boulder Lake. We were two miles away!

For an hour, wave after wave of snow geese passed overhead. Even if the geese had been within range of our guns, I doubt if we would have fired a shot. We all stood there with our mouths open. I don't know how many thousands of geese passed by, and it really doesn't matter. I'll never forget the "whoosh" of their wings and their constant honking. What music! That has to be among the most exciting sounds in nature.

Let's take a look at this grand, wild goose.

— M.E.A.

CHAPTER ONE:

A big family

All waterfowl, which includes geese, swans, and ducks, belong to one big family. Experts call this group of animals the *Anatidae* family. Across the world, there are almost 150 species, or different kinds, of waterfowl. By studying their habits and features, the experts group waterfowl into eleven "tribes."

The snow goose is one of the seven types of geese found in North America.

North America is home to more than forty of these species, which are split into seven tribes. All geese and swans are put into the tribe *Anserini*. In North America, there are four species of swans and seven species of geese. The geese include the white-fronted goose, emperor goose, barnacle goose, brant, Ross' goose, Canada goose, and the snow goose.

Geese have old ancestors

There have been geese in North America for a very long time. Unlike many other wild animals, experts think that ancestors of today's geese were able to live through the Ice Age. During the Ice Age, glaciers covered a large part of North America. It is thought that glaciers covered the land as far south as the Missouri and Ohio Rivers in the United States. From that southern border, ice covered the land almost to the northern edge of North America. Just where you would think the ice would be thickest, there were no glaciers. Some areas of land closest to the North Pole were free of ice.

The ice-free areas included the Bering Land Bridge, and parts of eastern Asia and Alaska that were joined by this narrow strip of land. Northern Greenland and some of the islands between Greenland and Alaska were also free of ice.

These small pieces of land in the Arctic provided the ancestors of today's geese with ideal nesting areas. The geese spent the summers in the Arctic raising their young. In the fall, they flew south across thousands of miles of ice-covered land. The geese spent the winter months in warmer areas south of the glaciers that covered northern North America. In the spring, these geese flew back to the Arctic.

The ability of the geese to fly across the glaciers is what allowed them to survive the Ice Age. Many other animals were trapped by the ice and became extinct. This may also explain why most present-day geese migrate each spring and fall, even if they don't have to. Their ancestors had to migrate to survive, and the habit has been passed on through the years.

Geese greet the first humans

Thousands of years ago the glaciers slowly melted. After the glaciers were gone, experts think that the first humans came to North America. These people came across the Bering Land Bridge from Asia. If they came during the spring or fall, they were, no doubt, greeted by some ancestors of today's snow geese flying over-

The first humans in North America would have seen flights of snow geese.

head. Depending on the season, the geese would have either been leaving or returning to their summer home in the far North.

In western North America, early Eskimos and Indians might have seen white geese with black wing tips. Later, in the center of North America they might also have seen the same white geese. But mostly, they would have seen geese that only had white heads. The bodies of these geese were bluish-gray in color. When humans got to eastern North America, they might have seen a relative of these white and "blue" geese. This eastern goose looked just like the white goose in western North America, only it was larger.

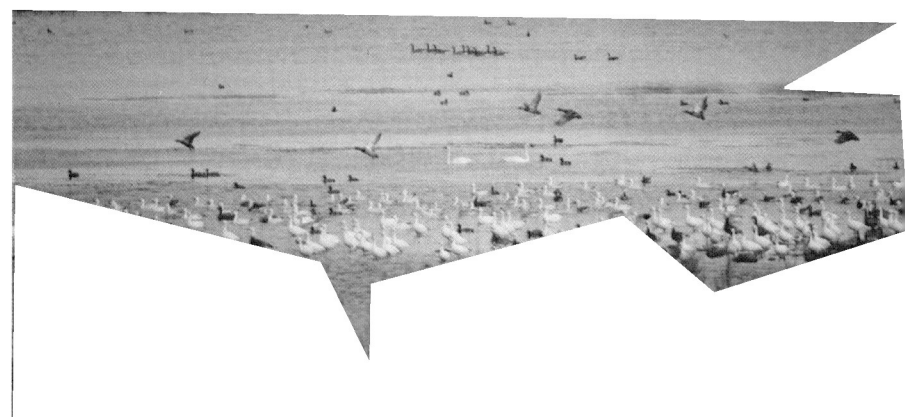

Both snow geese and Canada geese, shown on a Canadian marsh, lived through the Ice Age.

Finding names wasn't easy

The Eskimos living in the far North long ago began to depend on these different geese for food. They gathered and ate eggs that the geese laid in the spring. If they were going to eat a goose, they had to catch it by hand. That wasn't easy! The Eskimos didn't have weapons to kill the geese from a long distance. They didn't have bows and arrows to kill geese like the Indians living farther south. The Indians were able to eat both the geese and their eggs.

Although the Eskimos and Indians had their own names for these geese, they didn't much care about how the birds might be related to each other. It was only after white people came to North America in the late 1700's, that such details were studied

To try and explain what happened when the experts started naming these white and bluish-gray geese may only confuse you. Lifetimes have been spent trying to figure it out. Many books have been written on the subject. It took the experts about 150 years to sort through all the information.

Most experts now agree that there are only two separate species of light-colored geese in North America. One species is the Ross' goose, and the other is the snow goose.

Ross' goose — a close relative

From a distance, only the best experts can tell a Ross' goose from a white snow goose. Both geese are white with black wing tips. Up close, some things are easier to see. The Ross' goose is smaller. An adult seldom weighs more than four pounds (1.8 kg). Its neck is shorter, and its bill is not as long as the snow goose's. The Ross' goose often has wart-like bumps above its nostrils, while the snow goose doesn't. The Ross' goose also lacks the black outline found on the snow goose's bill.

The feet and legs of an adult Ross' goose are a rose-pink color. The same parts on snow geese are an orange-red color. An expert might also be able to notice the faster wing beat and more highly-pitched call of the Ross' goose. The proper name for the Ross' goose is *Anser rossii*.

The two types of snow geese

The experts have decided that there are two subspecies, or types, of snow goose. The larger type is called the greater snow goose *(Anser caerulescens atlantica)*.

The other type, being smaller, is called the lesser snow goose *(Anser caerulescens caerulescens)*.

The greater snow goose is all white, except for its black wing tips. The males and females look alike. Their bills are pink, and their legs and feet are orange-red in color. Sometimes there is a rust-colored stain on their white necks. The rusty stain is caused by iron that is often in the soil where they feed. Most adult males weigh about seven and-a-half pounds (3.4 kg). Adult females weigh about six pounds (2.7 kg).

The lesser snow goose comes in two colors. This makes it a very rare bird! In most cases, color is what sets one species of bird apart from another. As you will see, this is not true when it comes to the lesser snow goose.

This rare bird has two color "phases," or stages of development. Some lesser snow geese have dark plumage. This bird is better known as the "blue goose." Other lesser snow geese have light plumage. This is the goose that people call the plain-old "snow goose." But make no mistake about it — the experts have decided that they are the same bird.

It is thought that the different colors evolved thousands of years ago. The experts think that the white geese developed in a habitat filled with snow and ice. The "blue" geese, they think, first came from an area that had more exposed ground. In both cases, the geese developed colors that would help them hide from danger.

A white phase snow goose is surrounded by blue phase snow geese.

White phase and blue phase

At a quick glance, the white phase of the lesser snow goose looks just like the greater snow goose. The color of the feathers, bill, feet, and legs is the same. Males and females of the white phase also look alike. Males weigh about six pounds (2.7 kg), and the females weigh about five and-a-half pounds (2.5 kg).

The lesser snow goose, then, is only a little smaller than the greater snow goose. How do you tell them apart? You have to check the bill. The bill on the greater snow goose is bigger around. The bill is also longer on the greater snow goose. The easiest thing to check is the length of the bill. Both male and female greater snow geese will have a bill that is a little over two and-a-half inches (65 mm) long. Both sexes of the lesser snow goose have a bill that is only a little over two inches (55 mm) long.

The only thing that sets the blue phase apart from the white phase is the color of the plumage. Blue phase adults have white heads and upper necks. Their bodies are slate gray, except for white tail feathers. The wings are mostly light gray. The tips of the wings have black feathers like other snow geese. The color of the bill, legs, and feet of the blue phase geese is the same as those of the white phase. Adult males and females look alike, and weigh the same as the white phase adults.

Moves with the seasons

Like other kinds of geese, snow geese migrate, or move, with the seasons. They have two "homes." Most snow geese spend the winter months in the southern part of the United States or northern Mexico. The rest of the snow geese in North America are along the middle part of the East coast of the United States during the winter.

During the summer months, snow geese are found in the most northern areas of Asia and North America. They live in a narrow band from the northeast coast of Russia, across northern Canada, to the northwest coast of Greenland.

Like all waterfowl that migrate, the snow geese fly south in the fall and north in the spring.

Snow geese usually do not follow neat north-south lines when they migrate. They often move sideways. Because of this, it's hard to use the usual term, "flyways," to describe north-south movement of these waterfowl. Many years ago the four flyways were setup to control hunting. They were named (from West to East) the Pacific Flyway, the Central Flyway, the Mississippi Flyway, and the Atlantic Flyway. It was a useful way to divide states and provinces into four north-south areas to regulate hunting.

But the flyways often don't "work" when it comes to describing the movement of the snow goose. For example, a snow goose may leave northern Russia in the fall along the Pacific Flyway. When it gets to Alaska it might take a new course that will take it down the Central Flyway. Recent studies have also shown that waterfowl use different routes. When going south in

Thousands of snow geese gather in California during the winter months.

the fall, they follow one route. When going north in the spring they often follow another route.

Migration routes are changing

There is also another problem. For thousands of years geese used the same routes. They could be counted on to follow the same river while going south. Their trip north in the spring might be along another route, but it was the same year-after-year. Today, however, their routes are slowly changing from one year to another. Changing farming methods are the main cause. The

These snow geese found a field of harvested corn to feed in at sunset.

geese have changed their migration routes to take advantage of new food supplies.

Because of the changing pattern, no one can make perfect maps showing the routes the snow goose will follow when migrating. The best that can be done is to show general movement patterns. Keep that in mind when you look at the map on page 45.

Why snow geese migrate

There is one very big reason that snow geese, as well as most other waterfowl, migrate. The reason is survival. They would die if they didn't leave their breeding areas in the far North when winter came. When their breeding areas freeze over with ice and snow, they cannot get the two things they need to survive — food and water. They can't stay in their winter areas all year either. They would not have enough food or space to raise their young.

Experts think that waterfowl have an internal "clock" that tells them when it's time to migrate. They think that the rapidly changing hours of daylight in the spring and fall "trigger" the birds to migrate.

Changing weather also seems to have an effect. In the fall, a strong wind out of the north often causes a flock of snow geese to head south. A strong wind out of the south seems to have the same effect in the spring. It often starts the geese on their way north. It's as if the geese know that a strong wind will make it much easier for them to migrate. A strong tail wind allows them to conserve their energy for the long trip ahead.

How do they get where they're going?

Snow geese, like other waterfowl, are able to return to the same breeding and wintering areas each year. Bands of metal attached to the legs of snow geese have proven this. To check this, experts "band" several geese in a certain area. The bands are numbered. The numbers tell the experts where the goose was banded.

In later years, the experts hope to get back information in one of two ways. Hunters are asked to report where and when they shot a banded goose, along with the number on the band. The other way is for the experts to live-trap geese in areas where geese have been banded in the past. When they find a goose with a band, they check the number against a master list that shows where the goose was banded. At the same time, bands can be put on other geese. Over a number of years, the experts

An expert fastens bands to the legs of goslings.

can get a good idea of migration routes. They've also learned that the geese usually return to the same breeding and wintering areas year after year.

Great navigators

How do the geese do it? How do they travel thousands of miles, in all kinds of weather, without getting lost? Experts don't have all the answers, but they have learned many things about how the geese do it.

It is known that migrating waterfowl make use of the landscape when going across country. Large flocks of snow geese have been seen to change their course to follow a river, for example. They have also been seen following a coastline.

What happens on a dark night when the ground cannot be seen? Experts have been able to figure out that

Snow geese often follow waterways when they migrate.

snow geese and other waterfowl use the stars to help them "steer" a course on a clear night. They also think that waterfowl make use of the wind and the earth's magnetic field to guide them on a cloudy night.

These systems do not always work, however. On nights with heavy overcast, snow geese have been known to fly past an intended target. They were flying in the right direction, but flew too far. When this happens, the geese usually land and fly back after daylight.

Putting the pieces of the migration puzzle together has taken much effort and time. Bit by bit the experts are coming up with more answers. Someday they might figure it all out.

Breeding grounds of the lesser snow goose

There is only one reason that snow geese fly north in the spring. The areas they need for breeding and raising their young are in the far North. No other North American waterfowl flies as far north.

The lesser snow goose makes use of three main areas. These areas are Wrangel Island near Siberia, the north-

The snow goose flies further north than any other North American waterfowl.

ern coast of the Northwest Territories, and areas on the west and north sides of Hudson Bay.

As many as 400,000 lesser snow geese fly north along the western edge of North America to get to Wrangel Island. They usually leave their wintering areas in central and northen California in February. They make a number of stops along the way to rest and eat. The geese usually reach Wrangel Island during the last week in May. Most, if not all, of these geese are of the white phase.

Both blue phase and white phase lesser snow geese use the breeding areas of the Northwest Territories. Most of these geese come from wintering areas in southern California and northern Mexico. About 250,000 geese arrive in the area around the Mackenzie River delta and Banks Island during the first two weeks of May. These areas on the west end of the Northwest Territories have mostly white phase geese. Many lesser snow geese that go to the Victoria Island area of the Northwest Territories are blue phase geese.

About 1,500,000 lesser snow geese go to areas around Hudson Bay to breed. Most of these geese leave their winter areas along the Gulf Coast of the United States by early March. They usually arrive in their breeding areas during the last week of May and the first week of June.

The geese that breed on the west coast of Hudson Bay and Southhampton Island are a mixture of white and blue phase geese. The geese that go further north and east to the south coast of Baffin Island are almost all blue phase geese.

The western end of the lesser snow goose range has mostly white phase geese. The furthest area to the east has mostly blue phase geese. The middle of their range has a mixture of both. In areas where both types occur, they freely mate with each other.

When both types mate, the young are not "hybrids." They don't have a mixture of the colors of each parent like hybrids do. Instead, they are either a pure white phase or a pure blue phase goose. It's this last fact that led the experts to decide that both types were the same species. If some of the young were a mixture of both colors, it would have meant that they were separate species.

A blue phase goose watches over two goslings.

Breeding grounds of the greater snow goose

All of the greater snow geese in North America spend the winter in coastal areas of North Carolina, Virginia, Delaware, and Maryland. There are about 100,000 greater snow geese that migrate to their breeding

Greater snow geese spend their winters on the East coast of the United States.

grounds in late March or early April. After making a couple of long stops, they reach their breeding grounds in late May or early June. Most of them go to the north coast of Baffin Island and the north end of Ellesmere Island. A number of them go to the west coast of Greenland. The greater snow goose is one of the very few North American birds that nest on Greenland.

Winter areas of the snow goose

Almost all of the lesser snow geese go to one of two areas during the winter months. They either go to the coastal marshes of Texas and Louisiana, or they go to the inland marshes in California. In both of these areas, the geese are able to forage for waste grain in recently harvested fields.

Greater snow geese used to go mainly to the coastal marshes of North Carolina and Virginia. Today, there seem to be more of these geese in Delaware and Maryland. The geese have been attracted by the recent increase in the land being used to raise grain. The geese have learned that it is easier to forage for grain than to eat their usual foods. More will be mentioned about this in the section on food and feeding habits.

CHAPTER TWO:

Sharp senses

Canada geese are often thought to be among the wisest of all waterfowl. But it's possible that the snow goose is even more clever. Almost any person who has hunted for both of these geese will tell you that it is far more difficult to fool a snow goose.

The snow goose has excellent senses to help make it "wise." Like most waterfowl, it's eyes are very good. Because the eyes are on the side of its head, the snow goose can see in nearly a complete circle. The only "blind spot" is the area right behind its head. Snow geese are especially good at spotting any unnatural movement while flying high in the sky.

The snow goose's sense of hearing is also well developed. As early Eskimo and Indian hunters learned, it's almost impossible to sneak up on a snow goose. The smallest sound will alert an entire flock that is feeding or resting on the ground.

Experts do not think that the snow goose has a good sense of smell. This is probably because the snow goose doesn't need a good sense of smell. The snow goose needs only its eyes to spot food. Its senses of hearing and sight are usually enough to warn of danger.

The snow goose is always alert for danger.

31

Food and feeding habits

For thousands of years, the snow goose made use of the sharp edges of its bill. The sharp edges evolved over the years to clip off the roots of marsh plants, as well as Arctic plants and grasses. While on their breeding grounds in the Arctic, snow geese still feed the way they have done for a long time. They feed mainly on sedges, grasses, cranberry, salmonberry, curlewberry, and the shoots of three-square bullrushes.

On their Arctic breeding grounds, snow geese feed on grasses and plants.

Feeding habits change

On wintering grounds in the United States, snow geese were once fond of the roots of marsh plants like cordgrass and cattail. But in recent times their eating habits, while in their winter areas, began to change. The experts first noticed the change in California several decades ago.

In California, the snow geese began to shift from marsh plants to food produced by present-day farming methods. The geese began to feed on the grains of barley, wheat, and rice that were left in fields after farmers had finished harvesting. They also began to feed on the green shoots of the same grains in the spring. These crops soon became the main source of food everywhere in the West. Snow geese usually make one trip to the fields in the morning and one in the afternoon. Between times, they fly back to the marshes to rest or sleep.

These same eating habits soon spread to all wintering areas where there were large fields of grain crops. In Texas and Louisiana, snow geese favor the rice fields. When farmers in Maryland and Delaware switched from dairy farms to large-scale raising of grains, the snow geese also switched their habits. They moved from their traditional wintering areas in the coastal marshes of Virginia and North Carolina. They now spend their winters in the areas around Chesapeake Bay and

Delaware Bay. Instead of eating marsh plants, they fly to nearby fields of corn, soybeans, and wheat to forage for leftovers after the fall harvest. Like their "cousins" elsewhere, they also feed on the green shoots of grain crops in the spring.

Migration habits change, too

The snow geese have changed their migration routes to take advantage of the same food crops. For thousands of years, the migration routes had been centered on marshes where snow geese could find their favorite marsh plants. Today, the routes are centered on areas of water that are near large grain fields.

Snow geese have also slowed down their fall migrations to feast on the new food supply. This is most true in the "farm belt" of south-central Canada and the north-central United States. The snow geese are now found along the Missouri River in Iowa, Nebraska, Missouri, and Kansas as late as January. Years ago, snow geese didn't even stop in these areas unless bad weather forced them to do so. They used to fly over this area as early as November!

It's not hard to imagine why snow geese have changed their eating and migration habits. Where flocks of geese once looked down on a boring patchwork of small brown fields, they now see large, inviting areas that say "food." There are huge green fields of sprouting winter wheat, as well as large gold fields of picked corn and other grains.

Snow geese have also slowed down their migration to the North in the spring. They will often stop in sprouting fields of winter wheat. But in the spring, they can't delay too long. They have to get to their breeding grounds as early as possible. They don't have much time to raise their young before winter closes in on them.

Today, migration routes center on water that is near large fields of grain.

Snow geese usually start their migrations after sunset.

High flyers

Snow geese migrate in very large flocks. Flocks of up to one thousand are common. They usually start their migrations (both north and south) after sunset. They will often wait for a day that has a strong wind blowing in the direction they want to go. They prefer flying with the wind whenever possible.

Snow geese fly in a wide formation that is somewhat V-shaped. The "V" is not as sharply angled as that of a smaller flock of Canada geese. While Canada geese tend to fly straight ahead, flocks of snow geese fly in a wavering line. The formation often looks like a loosely-strung, beaded necklace. This flying habit gave rise to their nickname of "wavie."

Migrating snow geese fly at an average speed of fifty miles per hour (80 kph). They usually fly between two thousand and three thousand feet (610-915 m) above the ground. They are also found at twice that height. There is even one report of an airline pilot seeing snow geese at twenty thousand feet (6098 m)!

Spring is the time for mating

Snow geese begin to look for a mate during their second year. Mates are usually selected during the time spent in the wintering areas.

Snow geese usually mate for life. The pair usually do not breed until their third or fourth year of life. If a mate dies, a new mate is usually picked the following winter.

Actual mating is thought to take place during the late stages of the spring migration to the breeding grounds. Some pairs do not mate until they reach the breeding area.

When the flocks arrive on the breeding grounds, the ground is often covered with snow. As soon as the snow melts, the flocks break up into pairs. Each pair finds a patch of bare ground and strongly defends it. The male only defends their territory against male intruders, while the female only attacks other females.

Snow geese usually locate their nests within a few miles of the sea, along large rivers, or on islands in small lakes that are close to the sea. The nests begin as only scrapes in the tundra moss or gravel. Moss, willows, and grass are added to the nests as the eggs are laid. The female later adds a bit of down from her breast after she lays each egg. This helps keep the eggs warm.

Eggs are laid in June

As many as ten eggs, and as few as two eggs, are laid in each nest. The average nest will have four or

A male snow goose defends its nest!

five eggs. As soon as the last egg is laid, the female begins to incubate them. The female leaves the nest only to make short trips to get food. If the weather is very cold, the female never leaves the nest. This sometimes causes the female to starve to death, and the eggs don't hatch.

The male guards the nest against other snow geese, as well as predators, like the Arctic fox. The male charges intruders with stretched-out neck and wings,

A snow goose gosling leaves the nest soon after it is born.

calling loudly. If all goes well, the eggs hatch in about three weeks.

The group of chicks, called a "brood," is led away from the nest in a few days in search of food. Many broods have been seen as far as thirty miles (49 k) from their nest site. Within forty-five days, the young, called goslings, have lost their down and are completely feathered. Their first flights are usually made about ten days earlier. The geese spend almost all of their time grazing on Arctic grasses and plants. Within ninety days the young snow geese will weigh about five pounds (2.3 k), which makes them almost as large as their parents. This is also a time for the female to regain the weight that she lost while sitting on the nest. The family sleeps on the ground at night.

New feathers

About two weeks after the goslings are born, the adult snow geese "molt," or change, their feathers. During this three-week-long process, the snow geese lose their old feathers and grow new ones. The adults cannot fly while this change takes place. By the time the goslings are ready to take their first flights, the adults have their new feathers and are able to fly with them. All of the snow geese are ready to fly by late August, when they must begin their migration to the South. As the time to migrate comes near, the geese gather in large flocks along the seacoast. One day, with a great roar, and much honking, they'll start their trip to their wintering areas.

Enemies of the snow goose

The main natural predators of the snow goose are the Arctic fox, hawks, and eagles. These predators will steal eggs if they get a chance. They will also go after the young goslings if the parents are not around. Unless they are sick, the adults themselves are not often attacked by any of these predators.

Because snow geese are so spread out while on their summer breeding grounds, disease is not a big problem. In the wintering areas, however, snow geese can be killed by the thousands. This is because the geese are often packed together, and disease can spread. This usually happens when there is a lack of enough winter habitat.

Today, the shortage of wintering areas is what controls the numbers of snow geese at any one time in North America. There is room for many more geese on the breeding grounds. Concerned people are now working very hard to provide more places for snow geese to spend the winter months. Like all waterfowl, snow geese badly need more wetlands if they are going to thrive.

The Arctic fox is a predator of the snow goose.

The outlook is good

The change of farming methods has been good for both the Canada goose and the snow goose. (It has not been as good for other waterfowl, like ducks. As the land has been cleared, the little prairie potholes, that ducks need for raising their young, have disappeared.) The numbers of snow geese have been slowly increasing in recent years. There are so many snow geese in some areas, that farmers are starting to complain about crop losses. It's a nice situation when game management people have to worry about having too many geese. Not many years ago, no one could have imagined that this would be possible. If more wintering areas can be provided, the future looks bright, indeed, for the snow goose of North America.

The future looks bright for the snow goose.

MAP:

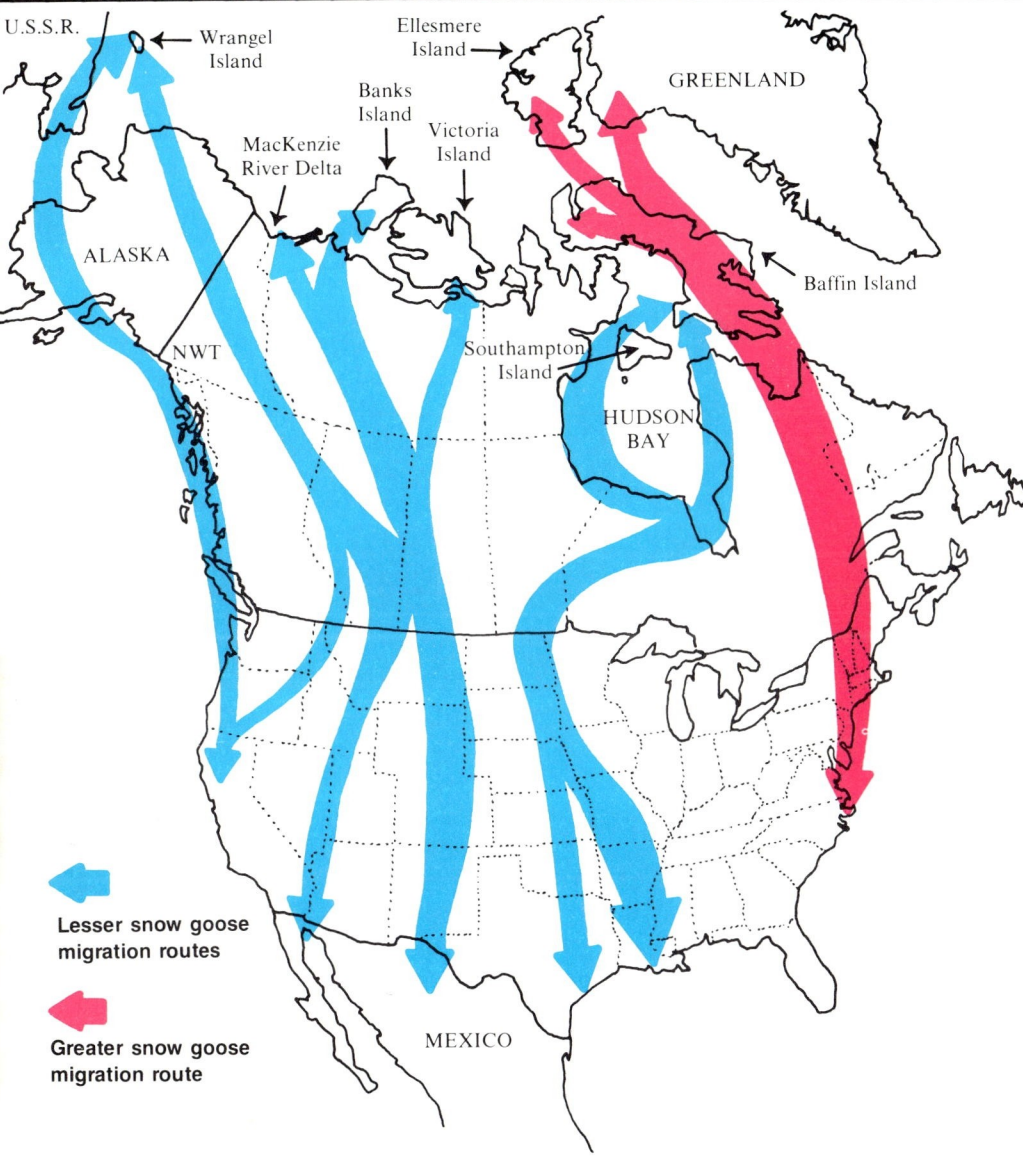

INDEX/GLOSSARY:

ANCESTOR 7, 8 — *A relative from long ago.*

BAND 20, 21 — *A strip of metal which is wrapped around the legs of waterfowl to check their movements.*

BERING LAND BRIDGE 7, 8 — *A strip of land that once connected Asia and North America in the area of Alaska.*

BROOD 41 — *A group of goslings.*

"BLUE GOOSE" 10, 13 — *The dark plumage phase of the lesser snow goose.*

BREEDING GROUNDS 19, 20, 21, 23, 26, 28, 29, 32, 35, 38, 42 — *The areas in the Arctic where the snow goose spends the summer months raising its young.*

COLORING 10, 12, 13, 15

DIET 32, 33, 34, 35, 41

DISEASE 42

ENEMIES 39, 42

EXTINCT 8 — *No longer living anywhere.*

EVOLVE 13 — *To slowly change in response to a changing habitat.*

FORAGE 29, 34 — *To feed on grasses and plants.*

GOSLINGS 21, 27, 40, 41, 42 — *The young of geese.*

HABITAT 13, 42 — *The surroundings and conditions in which an animal lives.*

HUNTING 4, 11, 20, 30

HYBRIDS 27 — *Offspring that show characteristics of both parents.*

INCUBATE 39 — *To keep eggs at the proper temperature until they hatch.*

LIVE-TRAP 20 — *To trap an animal without harming it.*

MATING 27, 37, 38, 39

MIGRATE 8, 15, 16, 18, 19, 20, 21, 22, 23, 26, 28, 34, 35, 36, 37, 38, 41 — *To move from one area to another.*

MOLT 41

PHASE 13 — *A stage in the development of an animal.*

PLUMAGE 13, 15 — *A bird's feathers.*

PREDATOR 39, 42, 43 — *An animal that eats other animals for food.*

RANGE 27 — *The large area in which an animal can naturally live.*

SENSES 30

SIZE 12, 13, 15, 41

INDEX/GLOSSARY:

SOUNDS 5, 12, 41, 42

SPECIES 6, 7, 11, 13, 27 — *A kind of animal that has features that make it different from other animals.*

SUBSPECIES 12 — *A group of animals that are closely related.*

TAIL WIND 20, 37 — *A wind blowing at the back of a flying object.*

TRIBE 6, 7 — *A group of people or animals with common ancestors.*

TUNDRA 38 — *A mostly flat, moss and grass-covered area of the Arctic.*

WATERFOWL 6, 16, 19, 20, 22, 23, 24, 30, 42, 44 — *A bird living in and around water that can swim.*

WINGS 12, 15

WINTERING AREAS 19, 20, 21, 26, 29, 33, 37, 42, 44 — *The areas in southern North America where snow geese spend the winter months feeding and resting.*

READ AND ENJOY THE SERIES:

If you would like to know more about all kinds of wildlife, you should take a look at the other books in this series.

You'll find books on bald eagles and other birds. Books on alligators and other reptiles. There are books about deer and other big-game animals. And there are books about sharks and other creatures that live in the ocean.

In all of the books you will learn that life in the wild is not easy. But you will also learn what people can do to help wildlife survive. So read on!